Doubt & Assurance

Doubt & Assurance

Edited by
R. C. Sproul

Ligonier
Ministries

BAKER BOOK HOUSE
Grand Rapids, Michigan 49516

Published by Baker Books,
a division of Baker Book House Company
P.O. Box 6287, Grand Rapids, Michigan 49516-6287

Printed in the United States of America

Library of Congress Cataloging-in-Publication Data

Doubt and assurance / edited by R. C. Sproul.
    p.   cm.
  ISBN 0-8010-8352-4
  Contents: The anatomy of doubt / R. C. Sproul — When doubt becomes unbelief / Alister McGrath — Doubt and the apologist / W. Andrew Hoffecker — I believe in doubt / Os Guinness — Doubt in the face of suffering / Sinclair Ferguson — Doubting God's goodness / R. Bruce Steward — Fear not / R. C. Sproul — The privilege of assurance / Roger Nicole — True and false assurance / John H. Gerstner — Assurance and sin / Ron Kilpatrick — How to know that you know him / Steve Brown — Assurance, a pastor's perspective / John Richard DeWitt.
    1. Faith. I. Sproul, R. C. (Robert Charles), 1939- .
  BT772.D68 1993
  231′.042—dc20   92-37764

The material contained in this book was originally published in *Tabletalk* Magazine and was compiled in this format by the editor of *Tabletalk*, Robert Ingram.

Contents

Part 2 *Assurance*

Preface

R. C. Sproul

I remember our high school senior prom. The school buzzed with excitement when it was announced that live entertainment would be provided by "The Smooth-Tones." The Smooth-Tones was a Rhythm-and-Blues singing group that made it briefly to the top of the charts with their hit record "No Doubt About It." The song celebrated the certainty that floods the heart of a boy in love.

Love—especially puppy love—admits to no uncertainty.

Few things, however, are met with such assurance and conviction. Many things that matter most to us are shrouded in the cloud of the dubious. To be sure about urgent matters, such as our health, our job security, our performance, is often a luxury that eludes us. We hope, but we are not sure.

This book explores doubt and certainty with regard to ultimate questions concerning the existence of God and especially our relationship with him.

We usually oscillate between the two poles of doubt and certainty. There are degrees of doubtfulness. I am not equally certain about everything I believe. To some questions I respond by saying, "I'm sure." But answers to other questions remain uncertain. The Bible itself allows for uncertainty in matters where God is silent; yet where God has spoken the matters are now certain. Nothing is more certain than that God cannot lie and cannot err. He is the ground basis for all genuine assurance. His Word may be attacked or denied, but never falsified.

I know of only two sources of absolute certainty: God and reason. The first source is denied by the atheist or agnostic. The second source is denied by irrationalists. God is the source of certainty because he is the infallible source of truth. Reason yields absolute certainty in a formal way.

Rational certainty operates through logical deduction within a framework of ideas or propositions. For example, if it is true that all men are mortal, and it is also true that Socrates is a man, then the conclusion "Socrates is mortal" is absolutely certain. This "certainty" of reason, however, rests on a formal relationship of propositions. We may question the propositions themselves but not the validity of the conclusion.

Premises are propositions that may be true or false. Arguments are not true or false; they are valid or invalid. Logic is a tool to determine the formal validity of those arguments. Through logic we can test that validity with absolute certainty. But keep in mind the limitations of this test. The concluding premise in an argument may be true while the argument is invalid. Or the conclusion may be false while the argument is valid.

For example we might argue:

> All fat animals are rats.
> Socrates is a fat animal.
> ∴ Socrates is a rat.

Here, the argument is formally valid though the conclusion is untrue because its premises are untrue.

But why introduce questions of logic and reason into a discussion about doubt and certainty? If God says it, doesn't that alone remove all doubt? Certainly there is no doubt about the truth of what God says. He is an infallible source. But in making that judgment I already am using reason to banish doubt. Someone else might say, "Just because God says it, doesn't make it true." If, however, we mean by God a Being who is infallible then we can say, "Indeed it does, because God is infallible, and whatever infallible beings say must be true."

Reason also enters at the level of understanding what God says. If God says, "Boojiems live on Mars," I may not know what Boojiems are, but I know they are alive and that they live on Mars. Then suppose God says, "If you believe in Jesus you will be saved." My reason is involved in an attempt to understand what it means to believe, what it means to be saved, and who it is who is called "Jesus."

This is simply to say that doubt and assurance are matters of the mind. My arm doesn't doubt anything. My foot has no convictions. My thumb understands nothing. I may have feelings in my stomach or other physical symptoms related to issues of doubt or assurance, but they flow from the mind, not apart from it. Assurance floods my heart and fills my soul only when my mind has been convinced of the truth.

This is why it is urgent that we fully apply our minds to the Word of God. Faith—and assurance—come from hearing, and hearing by the Word of God (see Rom. 10:17). We hear sounds with our ears. But before we can distinguish meaning the sounds must be processed by the mind. An ear severed from the mind hears and understands nothing.

Not all our beliefs are self-evident truths. Indeed, we can rest assured that error invades our thinking at many points.

If we knew which points we would dispense with error. Doubt can help lead us from error to truth. Doubt can be a vital tool for the achievement of assurance. To gain assurance of crucial truths often requires that we doubt premises we've accepted uncritically. Doubt forces us back to first principles.

Doubt does not, indeed cannot, exist in a vacuum. Without some knowledge I cannot doubt at all. It is in the light of truth that doubt becomes a possibility. But doubt cannot ever have the last word. Only truth can establish doubt. Truth demands that we doubt what does not conform to truth.

When we build our house on truths that are sure, then we can dwell in the comfort of assurance. It is the foundation that is most crucial. Only with a sound foundation can we safely and rightly say, "No doubt about it."

Contributors

Steve Brown is president and Bible teacher for Key Life Network, Inc., and professor of homiletics at Reformed Theological Seminary, Orlando, Florida. Among his books are *If God Is In Charge* and *When Being Good Isn't Enough.*

Dr. John Richard DeWitt is the senior pastor of Seventh Reformed Church in Grand Rapids, Michigan.

Dr. Sinclair Ferguson is professor of systematic theology at Westminster Theological Seminary–East in Philadelphia, Pennsylvania, and the author of several books, including *A Heart for God.*

Dr. John H. Gerstner is professor emeritus of church history at Pittsburgh Theological Seminary and Ligonier Ministries' professor-at-large. He recently wrote *The ABC's of Assurance* and a three-volume study of the theology of Jonathan Edwards.

Dr. Os Guinness, an author and speaker, lives in McLean, Virginia. He has recently authored *No God But God.*

Dr. W. Andrew Hoffecker is a professor of religion at Grove City College in Grove City, Pennsylvania. He is also coeditor of *Building a Christian Worldview.*

Rev. Ron Kilpatrick has pastored churches in West Virginia and Georgia and is currently on the pastoral staff of Coral Ridge Presbyterian Church in Fort Lauderdale, Florida.

Dr. Alister McGrath is professor of theology at Wycliffe Hall, Oxford University. His most recent popular books include *The Sunnier Side of Doubt* and *Cloud of Witnesses.*

Dr. Roger Nicole, retired from Gordon-Conwell Theological Seminary, now is visiting professor of theology at Reformed Theological Seminary in Orlando, Florida.

R.C. Sproul is chairman of Ligonier Ministries and professor of systematic theology and apologetics at Reformed Theological Seminary in Orlando, Florida. Among his twenty-eight books are *Before the Face of God, Book 1: A Daily Guide for Living from the Book of Romans.*

R. Bruce Steward has pastored churches in New Jersey, New York, and South Carolina. He is an associate pastor at Grace Baptist Church in Cape Coral, Florida.

Part 1

Doubt

1

The Anatomy of Doubt

R. C. Sproul

Spiritus sanctus non est skepticus—"The Holy Spirit is not a skeptic."

So Luther rebuked Erasmus of Rotterdam after Erasmus expressed disdain for Luther's statement that one could be confident in the truth of an assertion. Luther roared, "The making of assertions is the very mark of the Christian. Take away assertions and you take away Christianity. Away now with the skeptics!"

Doubt is the hallmark of the skeptic. The skeptic dares to doubt the indubitable. Even demonstrable proof fails to persuade. The skeptic dwells on Mount Olympus, far aloof from the struggles of mortals who care to pursue truth.

But doubt has other faces. It is the assailant of the faithful, striking fear into the hearts of the hopeful. Like Edith Bunker, doubt asks:

"Are you sure? . . .
"Are you *sure* you're sure?"

Doubt nags the soul. Still, doubt can appear as a servant of truth. Indeed, it is the champion of truth when it wields its sword against what is properly dubious. It is a citadel against credulity. Authentic doubt has the power to sort out and clarify the difference between the certain and the uncertain, the genuine and the spurious.

Consider René Descartes. In his search for clear, distinct, certain ideas he employed the application of a rigorous and systematic doubt process. He endeavored to doubt everything he could possibly doubt. He doubted what he saw with his eyes and heard with his ears for he realized that our senses can and do often deceive us. He doubted authorities, both civil and ecclesiastical, knowing that recognized authorities can be wrong. He would submit to no *fides implicitum* claimed by any human being or institution. Biographies usually declare that Descartes was a Frenchman, but his works reveal that he was surely born in Missouri.

Descartes doubted everything he could possibly doubt until he reached the point where he realized there was one thing he couldn't doubt. He could not doubt that he was doubting. To doubt that he was doubting was to prove that he was doubting. No doubt about it.

From that premise of indubitable doubt, Descartes appealed to the formal certainty yielded by the laws of immediate inference. Using impeccable deduction he concluded that doubt required thought. From there it was a short step to his famous axiom: *Cogito ergo sum,* "I think, therefore I am."

At last Descartes arrived at certainty, the assurance of his own personal existence. This was, of course, before David Hume attacked causality and Immanuel Kant argued that the self belongs to the unknowable noumenal realm that requires a "transcendental apperception" (whatever that is) to affirm at all. One wonders how Descartes would have responded to Hume and Kant had he lived long enough to deal with them. I have no doubt that the man of doubt would have prevailed.

When assailed by doubt, it is time to search diligently for first principles that are certain.

Clearly there were unstated assumptions lurking beneath the surface of Descartes' thought processes. One assumption was the existence of logic itself. The conclusion that to doubt doubt is to prove doubt is born of logic. It assumes the validity of the law of noncontradiction. If the law of noncontradiction is not a valid and necessary law of thought, then one could argue (irrationally) that doubt can be doubt and not be doubt at the same time and in the same relationship.

The second assumption was the validity of the law of causality, which is merely an extension of the law of noncontradiction. Descartes could not doubt that an effect *must* have an antecedent cause. Doubt, by logical necessity, requires a doubter, even as thought requires a thinker. This is simply arguing that no action of any kind can proceed from nonbeing. Hume's skepticism of causality was cogent insofar as he brilliantly displayed the difficulty of assigning a particular cause to a particular effect or event. But not even Hume was able to repeal the law of causality itself. It is one thing to doubt what the cause of a particular effect is; it is quite another to argue that the effect may have no cause at all.

Countless thinkers have made this error since Hume. I once read a critical review of my book *Classical Apologetics* in which the able and thoroughly Christian reviewer observed, "The problem with Sproul is that he refuses to acknowledge the possibility of an uncaused effect." I wrote to my reviewing colleague and pleaded guilty to the charge. *Mea culpa.* I do refuse to acknowledge even the most remote possibility of an uncaused effect. I have the same obstreperous stubbornness regarding circles that are not round and married bachelors. I asked my friend to cite one example, real or theoretical, of an uncaused effect and I would repent in dust and ashes.

I'm still waiting for his reply. If he reads this perhaps it will jog his memory and induce him to deliver the goods or admit his glaring error.

I certainly allow for uncaused being, namely God, but not for uncaused effects. An uncaused effect is an oxymoron, a veritable contradiction in terms, a statement so patently and analytically false that Descartes could refute it in his Dutch oven without the benefit of empirical testing.

So how does this affect the Christian who struggles with the doubts that assail faith? The content of Christianity, in all its parts, cannot be reduced simplistically to Cartesian syllogisms. The lesson we learn from Descartes is this: When assailed by doubt it is time to search diligently for first principles that are certain. We build upon the foundation of what is sure.

This search is a matter of consequence that affects the whole structure of apologetics. It seems astonishing that anybody would go to the extremes Descartes insisted on, simply to discover that he existed. What could be more self-evident to a conscious being than one's own self-consciousness? But Descartes was not on a fool's errand. In a world of sophisticated skepticism Descartes sought to establish a foundation of certainty that could uphold much, much more than one proposition. He moved from the certitude of self-consciousness to the certitude of the existence of God—no small matter for the doubt-ridden believer. Descartes and others like him understood that one must prove the existence of God before affirming the trustworthiness of Scripture and the birth and work of the person of Christ. Once it is certain that God exists and reveals himself in Scripture, there is ground for a legitimate *fides implicitum.*

But the order of the process used to destroy doubt is crucial. For example, the miracles of the Bible cannot prove , and were never designed to prove, the existence of God. The very possibility of a miracle requires that there first be a God who can empower it. It is not the Bible that proves the existence of God; it is God who, through miracle, attests that the Bible is his Word. Once the necessity of a self-revealing God is proven, belief in the Bible becomes implicitly a virtue.

The most important certainty we can ever have is the foundational certainty of the existence of God. It is this matter that prompted Edwards to declare: "Nothing is more certain than that there must be an unmade and unlimited being" (*Miscellanies*, # 1340).

On this bedrock of certainty rests the promises of that unmade, unlimited Being. On these promises we rest our faith. Doubting served Descartes well, but Edwards knew that ultimately, it is dubious to doubt the indubitable.

2

When Doubt Becomes Unbelief

Alister McGrath

Doubt is not unbelief. It can, however, *become* unbelief. That basic principle should guide our thinking as we differentiate doubt, which is natural within faith, from unbelief, which is not.

Doubt comes about because of our human weakness and frailty. We lack the confidence to trust fully in God and long for certainty in all matters of faith. But absolute certainty is hard to come by. You can be sure that $2 + 2 = 4$, but is that going to change your life? Is that going to give you a reason to live and hope in the face of death? And it isn't just Christians who are in this situation. The atheist's belief that there is no God is just as much a matter of faith as your belief that there is! Doubt also comes about through our lack of humility. All of us are tempted to believe that, because we haven't got the answers to the hard questions of faith, there aren't any answers to those questions.

We need to learn to be relaxed about doubt. Doubt is like an attention-seeking child. The more attention you pay to it, the more attention it demands. By worrying about our doubts we get locked into a vicious cycle of uncertainty.

So how does doubt become unbelief? Unbelief is the decision to live life as if there is no God. It is a deliberate decision to reject Jesus Christ and all that He stands for. But doubt is something quite different. Doubt arises within the context of faith. It is a wistful longing to be sure of the things in which we trust. But it is not, and need not become, a problem. Just because I can't prove my faith in God doesn't mean that it is wrong.

But unbelief can creep in during those moments of doubt. How? Think of faith as a lifeline to God like an umbilical cord, providing a channel through which his life-giving grace can reach you. Sever that link and faith will wither, just as a branch that is broken off a vine shrivels and dies (John 15:1–6). Have you read C. S. Lewis's *Screwtape Letters?* If you have you will remember how Lewis points out that Satan uses ploy after ploy to try to get Christians to break their links with God. Doubt is one of those ploys.

Think through what will happen if Satan can manage to get you obsessed with your doubts. You become introverted, looking inwards at yourself and your state of mind. You stop looking outwards from yourself to the promises of God that are confirmed and sealed through the death and resurrection of Christ. The more you worry about your doubts the less you look to God. Gradually, those vital links with the life-giving grace of God will wither—and your spiritual life will wither and shrivel. You will have allowed doubt to become unbelief by feeding doubts and starving faith. But feed your faith and the doubts will starve. Doubt is a problem that finally grows to become unbelief if—and only if—you allow it.

Unbelief thus comes about through three possible routes:

First, unbelief can be nurtured by *an unrealistic attitude to faith*. If you believe that you can, or need to, know everything with absolute certainty, your faith will encounter difficulties very soon. Faith isn't a product of absolutely certain knowledge. Faith is about being willing to live through trust in the existence and promises of God, knowing that one day his existence and those promises will be totally vindicated. But for the moment, we walk by faith, not by sight.

> *Doubt is like an attention-seeking child. The more attention you pay to it, the more attention it demands.*

Second, unbelief may come through *a morbid preoccupation with doubt*, by which you become so obsessed with your own mental states and your feelings that God is shut out of your life. Give God some breaks by looking outward, not inward. Look to the promises of God; savor them; accept them. Stop allowing doubts to dominate. Doubt, seen properly, is just the darker side of faith; rediscover the "sunnier side of doubt" (Tennyson)—the joy of faith itself.

Third, unbelief may come through *an immature faith*—a faith that refuses to grow up. Weak faith is vulnerable faith. The process of maturing as a Christian involves deepening our understanding of what we believe.

As we grow in maturity we are meant to deepen our understanding of faith. The things that bothered us when we were young in faith don't bother us quite so much. In fact, I now realize that most of my own early doubts simply reflected an inadequate understanding of my faith. As I grew older I grew wiser through reading, thinking, and listening to wise Christians. Understanding reinforces faith in much the same way steel reinforces concrete. Together, they can withstand far greater stress than they could ever withstand on their own.

When does doubt become unbelief? Answer: When you let it, by clinging to unrealistic ideas about faith, by getting hopelessly preoccupied with the doubts that are a natural part of the Christian life, or by failing to allow faith to grow. These pitfalls can all be avoided. Don't feel ashamed about your doubts. Talking them through with older and wiser Christians can be a vital safety valve that releases a head of doubting steam—a head of steam which could eventually lead from normal doubt to the hopelessness of unbelief.

3

Doubt and the Apologist

W. Andrew Hoffecker

Doubt is to a Christian apologist what *choke* is to a professional athlete and *block* to a best-selling novelist. You expect Michael Jordan to score with seconds on the clock and Tom Clancy to write as deadlines approach. You would likewise expect C. S. Lewis to radiate unflinching certainty against verbal attacks on Christianity. Unfortunately, life does not always conform to the ideal. If choking is commonplace in athletes and writer's block freezes untold authors, are apologists immune to doubt?

A case in point is the story of Lewis's activity in the Oxford Socratic Club. Established with Lewis's encouragement in

1941, the Socratic boasted of being Oxford's second largest student organization during the 1940s. Upwards of 80 enthusiastic undergraduates crowded together from 8:15 to 10:30 on Monday evenings. Their purpose was unabashedly intellectual—to debate the pros and cons of Christianity.

The format called for an opening attack or defense of Christian belief—the problem of evil, arguments for the existence of God, or Christ's claims of deity—followed by rebuttal. In an article entitled "Founding of the Oxford Socratic Club" Lewis articulated the society's raison d'être: Debaters were to obey Socrates' exhortation to "follow the argument wherever it led them." Lewis and his friends believed that, while participants harbored prejudices, arguments did not. Honest debates thrived on argument which, being impartial, had a life of its own.

The professor's own participation in the presentations highlighted the evenings. His mere presence guaranteed that intellectual doubt would diminish and orthodox Christian belief would prevail. As president of the club Lewis had the honor of first response to the invited guest—he was David, fully armed with logic and wit to slay an unsuspecting Goliath. A master of repartee, Lewis engaged in lively debate with some of the most famous critics of Christianity. To the enormous delight of his followers, Lewis unstintingly defended even the most difficult doctrines, then launched effective counterattacks against opposing views.

But on February 2, 1948, Lewis met his match, perhaps more. Nor was his antagonist in atheist or agnostic garb. Elizabeth Anscombe, a Catholic philosopher, attacked major points in Lewis's argument in chapter 3 of *Miracles*, "The Self-Contradiction of the Naturalist." Anscombe and Lewis shared many characteristics, both in mind and personality, which admirably suited them to public debate. Both loved mental battle, if not verbal swaggering, essential qualities to survive in the Socratic forum.

The evening became legendary as the most exciting and dramatic of the Socratic's twelve-year history. Supporters on both sides claimed victory, including (according to selective reports) both combatants. But Lewis scholars now differ radically in assessing the debate and its affect on Lewis. Several of his associates later described his and their spirits in gloomy detail, claiming that Lewis admitted defeat and became very depressed. A pupil confided to his diary that Lewis's description of the debate, employing his usual graphic imagery, "was all of the fog of war, the retreat of infantry thrown back under heavy attack." George Sayer said that Lewis conceded he was "proved wrong, that his argument for the existence of God had been demolished." Hugo Dyson, a member of the apologist's small group of friends known as the "Inklings," said shortly afterward, "Very well. . . . Now he had lost everything and was come to the foot of the cross."

Athletes choke, writers suffer from blocks, and apologists doubt.

Other accounts are much less dramatic. Lewis claimed to Walter Hooper, his secretary, that he had not been defeated, though Hooper added that Lewis revised the chapter in *Miracles* for the 1960 Fontana edition. Richard Purtill said that Lewis may have been "nonplused at the vigor of her attack and its source, since as a Catholic she might have been expected to be an ally." Interestingly, Anscombe herself supports this contention in her *Collected Papers* published thirty-five years later. Playing down the affair, she recounted the pro-

ceedings as a "sober discussion" of philosophical issues after
which Lewis reworked the chapter. As for the rather "odd"
exaggerated accounts by friends of Lewis's low spirits, she
characterized their remarks "as an interesting example of the
phenomenon called 'projection.'"

Since post mortem accounts differ, it is almost impossible
to ascertain exactly Lewis' state of mind or seeds of doubt
immediately after the events. At a minimum he altered his
argument to account for Anscombe's criticisms. Whether, or
how strongly, his faith faltered is somewhat open to question.

Fortunately, Lewis himself advised apologists of the
unusual mental states they should anticipate in the line of
duty. Accounts of the Lewis–Anscombe debate's repercussions
approximate what he described when he wrote "Founding of
the Oxford Socratic Club" as occupational hazards of defending Christianity. Because apologists are more than merely
rational beings, and because no one knows with absolute certainty where ideas will lead, apologetic discourse involves more
than a systematic argument. Apology also entails risk. All who
defend faith open themselves to opponents' fire, but risk
extends beyond enduring retaliatory attacks. "Worse still," he
tellingly admits, "we expose ourselves to the recoil from our
own shots: for if I may trust my personal experience, no doctrine is, for the moment, dimmer to the eye of faith than that
which a man has just successfully defended."

In another classic essay, "Christian Apologetics," Lewis
further probed the potential backwash of contending for the
faith. He warned that nothing is so dangerous to one's faith
as making a successful defense in the apologist's arena. Doubt
and pride, strange companions, pry their way into the psyche.
In the moment of victory, the apologist is tempted to believe
that Christianity's validity rests upon the apologist. If that

prideful notion is true then faith "seems no stronger than that weak pillar [the apologist]."

Then Lewis turns abruptly pastoral. Defenders take their lives as well as their arguments into battle. Apologists' only sure defense consists in "falling back continually from the web of our own arguments, as from intellectual counters, into the Reality—from Christian apologetics into Christ himself."

Lewis then concludes with a plea: "That also is why we need one another's continual help—*oremus pro invicem* (Let us pray for each other)."

Here, as in many other instances, Lewis displays a delicate balance between objective and subjective elements. Faith and doubt evidence both mental and emotional components. He expressed in poetic form the same idea in "The Apologist's Evening Prayer":

> From all my lame defeats
>   and oh! much more
> From all the victories
>   that I seemed to score;
> From cleverness shot forth
>   on Thy behalf
> At which, while angels weep,
>   the audience laugh;
> From all my proofs
>   of Thy divinity,
> Thou, who wouldst give no sign,
>   deliver me.
> Thoughts are but coins.
>   Let me not trust, instead
> Of Thee, their thin-worn
>   image of Thy head.
> From all my thoughts, even from
>   my thoughts of Thee

> O thou fair Silence, fall,
>   and set me free.
> Lord of the narrow gate
>   and the needle's eye,
> Take from me all my trumpery
>   lest I die.

Apologists are not different from others who live under
the effects of the Fall. Athletes choke, writers block, and apologists doubt. Lewis admitted his frailty and warned others
lest they not understand.

4

I Believe in Doubt

Using Doubt to Strengthen Faith

Os Guinness

Faith is much more than the absence of doubt, but an understanding of doubt is a key to a strong faith, a sound mind, and a quiet heart. Yet more confusions surround doubt than many Christian believers realize. C. S. Lewis spoke of two equal and opposite errors into which Christians are inclined to fall when thinking about doubt:

On the one hand, those who are theologically liberal tend to be too soft on doubt, lionizing such notions as *ambiguity* and *uncertainty*. This spiritual permissiveness becomes a slipway to unbelief. On the other hand, those who are theologically conservative tend to be too hard on doubt, demonizing the dire consequences of unresolved doubt and verging on a spiritual perfectionism that leaves doubters in such a state of guilt or despair they dare not acknowledge their doubts to others or even to themselves.

In the Scriptures, by contrast, we find a realistic yet healthy view of doubt as definitely serious but not terminal. Understood properly, this biblical view sees the role of doubt as constructive to belief. "I believe in doubt" is, therefore, far more than a roundabout way of saying that there is not believing without doubting so that "even in doubting, I believe." A bold Christian affirmation is that, because faith in Christ is true and fears no question or challenge, doubt can be a stepping stone to a tougher, deeper faith. In this sense, as George Mac-Donald asserted, doubts are "messengers of the Living One to the honest."

Here are three tips for followers of Christ who wish to have a view of doubt that strengthens faith: (1) Remember the character of doubt; (2) learn to resist its confusion, and (3) uncover and confront doubt's real causes.

First, *remember the character of doubt.* Contrary to widespread misunderstanding, doubt is not the same as unbelief, so it is not the opposite of faith. Rather it is a state of mind in suspension between faith and unbelief. To believe is to be of one mind in accepting something as true; to disbelieve is to be of one mind in rejecting it; to doubt is to waver somewhere between the two, and thus to be of two minds. This important distinction uncovers a major misconception of doubt—the idea that a believer betrays faith and surrenders to unbelief by doubting.

This twoness or doubleness represents the deepest dilemma of doubt. The heart in doubt is a divided heart. Here is the essence of the biblical view of doubt, which is echoed in human language and experience from all around the world. All of the New Testament words for doubt—for example, *dipsychos*, *diakrinō*, *distazō*, *dialogizoma*, and *meteōrizomai*—have this sense of doubleness. So also do many other languages. The Chinese speak of a person with "a foot in two boats" and the Navajo Indians of "that which is two with a person."

An all-important difference exists, therefore, between the open-minded uncertainty of doubt and the closed-minded certainty of unbelief. Because faith is crucial, doubt is serious. But because doubt is not unbelief it is not terminal. It is a halfway stage that can lead on to a deepened faith as easily as it can break down to unbelief.

The doubleness or indecision of doubt can be described from the outside with high-noon clarity. But from the inside it is foggy, gray, and disorienting. The world of doubting feels like a world with no landmarks and no bearings. Thus a second tip for those who want to develop a view of doubt that strengthens faith is: Learn to anticipate and resist the confusions of doubt.

Because doubt is not unbelief, it is not terminal. It is a halfway stage that can lead on to a deepened faith as easily as it can break down to unbelief.

Followers of Christ are not simply fair-weather believers. They are realistically committed to truth, people who "think in believing and believe in thinking" as Augustine expressed it. They are, therefore, like experienced pilots who can fly in bad weather as easily as in good, by night as well as by day, and upside down as well as right side up. Faith's rainy days will come and go and dark nights of the soul may threaten to overwhelm, but safe flying is possible for those who have a solid grasp of the instruments (God's truth and promises) and a canny realism about the storm and stress of doubt.

Many common confusions about doubt can be cleared away with help. For example, doubt is confused with unbelief, which reinforces doubtfulness by adding guilt. Others divorce faith from knowledge. Knowledge becomes assigned strictly to the realm of certainty and faith to uncertainty. There is the confusion of thinking that, because God is the answer to all doubt, only answers that are theologically correct "God-talk" are sufficient. Such confusions are an aggravation of the doubt, not its real source.

The first two tips for handling doubt are vital but obviously preliminary. Without remembering the character of doubt, any outbreak of uncertainty can call faith into question before doubt ever specifically doubts anything. Without resisting doubt's confusion, the symptoms can sidetrack a serious investigation of the root causes. But when these two steps have been followed the real job remains—the believer must tackle those root causes. The third tip for those who want to strengthen faith through doubt is that they must *resolve the specific challenges that underlie it.*

Any attempt to draw up an exhaustive catalog of doubts would be overwhelming and depressing. But anyone who listens to doubters and studies doubt in the light of the Scriptures soon finds that there are "family resemblances" among doubts. It is, therefore, possible and helpful to discern a broad overview of the main types. Of course, these broad "families" are only generalizations. Doubting is specific, and doubts strike everyone differently. But, when used with sensitivity and compassion, the categories are anything but a straitjacket. They help people to see where they are, how they got there, and—most importantly—how they can get out.

It has been my privilege to talk to hundreds of individuals who have experienced different kinds of doubt and differing levels of pain and confusion. No one who understands the pain and perils of doubt can be blithe about it. Loss of trust in God is truly life's ultimate loss. But such is the nature of faith in God through Christ, affirmed by countless Christians through history, that there can be a constructive side of doubt.

True, there is no believing without some doubting. But since belief strengthens as the Christian understands and resolves doubt, we can say that, if we doubt in believing, we nevertheless also believe in doubting.

5

Doubt in the Face of Suffering

Sinclair Ferguson

To doubt is to be uncertain about God and to feel isolated from him; to suffer is to experience pain and to feel isolated from others. Giant Despair thus appears and imprisons us in what Bunyan aptly called "Doubting Castle." There, alone in the darkness, we begin to hear and believe the voices that say "there is no help for him in God" (Ps. 3:2 KJV).

But it is not true that there is no help for us in God! Hear the testimony of others: "Because the Sovereign Lord helps me, I will not be disgraced" (Isa. 50:7); "God is our refuge and strength, an ever-present help in trouble. . . . God will help . . . at break of day" (Ps. 46:1, 5).

The problem for the doubting sufferer, however, is that "break of day" has not yet come. It is still dark. When doubt is at its height and attacks most fiercely we ask, "Is there no light to help me through the night?"

Indeed there is; but the prescribed antidote tends to work slowly. It is important for us, therefore, to complete the course.

Scripture's account of genuine spiritual experience speaks to your situation. It describes your symptoms and illustrates the way of recovery. You are not unique. There is no test of faith that seizes us "except what is common to man. And God is faithful; he will not let you be tempted beyond what you can bear" (1 Cor. 10:13). Great saints of God have been where you are now.

Think of Elijah, suffering from total exhaustion; he doubted God's future purpose for his life and lay down to die. "I have had enough, Lord," he said (1 Kings 19:4). Here is Jeremiah, bravely facing being beaten and put in the stocks; he is a different man in private when the suffering catches up with him and he cries out, "O Lord, you deceived me, and I was deceived" (Jer. 20:7). There is John the Baptist, fearless in denouncing Herod's immoral behavior yet he receives an unwelcome visit from doubt as he languishes in prison and anxiously sends to know whether Jesus really is the Messiah after all (Luke 7:19).

Christian biography tells the same story. The great Scottish preacher Robert Bruce was often heard to say quietly, "It is a great thing to believe in God." Those who knew him well believed his confession was an expression of the enormous struggles of his soul. Illustrations, ancient and modern, could be multiplied. You are not alone; your experience is not altogether abnormal. As soon as you realize that, you will be assured that the divine medicine has been thoroughly field-tested. Indeed, the knowledge that your condition has been cured in the past will itself act on your spirits like a medicine.

Listen when Scripture offers the divine diagnosis and remedy for your experience. Our instinct, spiritually as well as physically, is to want an instant cure. But the providence of God is sometimes no clearer immediately in these experiences than when it comes time to choose a career or a marriage partner. Learn, therefore, to have a clear grasp of first principles and apply them to your own particular situation. To do so you must become familiar with the biblical teaching on the significance of suffering, and fit our own lives into its framework. As you do so, instead of doubting the goodness or the power of God, you will begin to marvel at the wisdom of his ways.

First, suffering is the result of the fall, the expression of a cosmos and a human race out of tune with its Creator. If doubt arises because we cannot understand "why bad things happen to good people" we need to have our thinking radically reoriented to Scripture. For there we learn that there are no "good people" (compare Gen. 8:21 with Rom. 3:9–18).

> *He who is himself at rest in the storm has his reasons: He means to display his glory and in his own time to say "Peace, be still," either to our circumstances or to our hearts.*

We belong to a fallen and sinful world. The real mystery is that good things happen to bad people. The recognition that God has done good to and for a sinful person like me in such a world as this is medicine that immediately begins to work.

Second, our suffering as Christians is part of what the New
Testament calls the divine *paideia* or child-training (Heb.
12:5–7, 11). It is not pleasant while we experience it; but after-
wards we can see that our Father was training and strength-
ening us through these disciplines. He sometimes works
painfully in our lives; he *always* works purposively, even if that
purpose becomes clear only later. As the Puritan John Flavel
once wrote, the providences of God are like Hebrew words—
they can only be read backwards.

So long as we know that the Father's hand directs even
suffering for our good (Rom. 8:28), we will not lose heart. For
the discipline of suffering then becomes a sign of true son-
ship (Heb. 12:5–12). Rather than cause us to doubt the Father
it leads us to ask him to fulfill the purposes of his love.

Third, suffering is a divine investment in our lives. It is the
raw material out of which God creates glory (2 Cor. 4:17). Part
of the reason for Paul's own suffering—as he later realized—
was to enable him to comfort others with the comfort which
he had experienced himself (2 Cor. 1:4). That is not the whole
story, of course, but it is an important part. Samuel Ruther-
ford put it quaintly: "Some graces grow best in winter."

Fourth, suffering may also be given to us to chasten and
humble us. Whatever Paul's "thorn in the flesh" was, he says
it "was given me" (2 Cor. 12:7). That phrase invariably points
to God's sovereign purpose, in this case, "to keep me from
becoming conceited." The scalpel of suffering had to be seen
in its proper context if it was to be understood. Paul needed
spiritual surgery. The heavenly Surgeon was cutting away the
potentially malignant growth of pride; this operation was a
"pridectomy"!

Fifth, sometimes our suffering is an aspect of a spiritual
conflict between the kingdom of God and the kingdom of darkness. That was so in the case of Job. Like Paul, his suffering

was "a messenger of Satan" (see Job 2:3–8); its purpose was to torment (literally, "to strike with the fist," 2 Cor. 12:7). Satan's design is always to make capital out of our suffering by producing doubts. "This proves God does not care for you" he whispers. "You are dispensable to him," he adds. Remember Job's wonderful response? "Though he slay me, yet will I trust him" (Job 13:15 NKJV). Seen in that light our suffering will make us determined to resist Satan, "standing firm in the faith" as Peter urges (1 Pet. 5:8–9).

Sixth, ultimately God's purpose in our suffering is to show us Christ's glory. Like the disciples in the storm on the Sea of Galilee we may wonder why he has brought us into such circumstances and cry out, "Don't you care if we drown?" (Mark 4:38). But he who is himself at rest in the storm has his reasons: He means to display his glory and in his own time to say "Peace, be still" (Mark 4:39 NKJV), either to our circumstances or to our hearts.

Paul discovered this when the Lord told him "My grace is sufficient for you, for my power is made perfect in weakness." Knowing this the apostle was able even to rejoice in his sufferings because in his weakness it would become clear that his strength lay only in Christ (2 Cor. 12:9–10; see Rom. 5:1–5). Paul might not be able to see the final tapestry God was weaving in his life, but he had a sight of the pattern the Master Weaver was using. That was enough to nourish his faith.

When we experience suffering, whether it is physical, mental, or emotional, most of us have a tendency to listen to the doubts and fears which ordinarily lie latent in our souls. One of the great lessons the Psalms teach us is that we must learn to speak back to our souls, to expound biblical teaching to them. We must exhort them to think biblically about our situation, dispensing the medicine Scripture prescribes. Then

we will learn to talk like the psalmist—as a true believer in the
face of both doubt and suffering:

> Why art thou then cast down, my soul?
>   what should discourage thee?
> And why with vexing thoughts
>   art thou disquieted in me?
> Still trust in God; for him to praise
>   good cause I yet shall have:
> He of my count'nance is the health,
>   my God that doth me save.
>   [Ps. 43:5, Scottish metrical version]

6

Doubting God's Goodness

A Pastor's Perspective

R. Bruce Steward

The prevalence of doubt in the lives of God's children seems strange. Doubt is the antipole of the life of faith, yet it is common among believers. In fact, faith and doubt coexist in their experience (Matt. 14:3; 28:17; Luke 12:28–29). Because of "the remains of sin," doubt is a fact of life, differing from Christian to Christian only in frequency, degree, or length of experience.

Most of the passages in the New Testament where the word *doubt* occurs refer to the believer. This underscores the need to deal with doubt when it arises. It may come in times of financial difficulty, change of situation, bodily affliction, loss of a loved one, temptation, or persecution. In such times God's faithfulness to keep his promises (1 Kings 8:15, 56; 1 Cor. 10:13) may be forgotten, or dismissed. God has promised to the faithful: (1) the necessities of life without anxiety (Matt. 6:25–34); (2) good things of life with persecutions (Mark 10:28–30), and (3) conquest in all difficulties (Rom. 8:35–39).

> *Because of "the remains of sin," doubt is a fact of life, differing from Christian to Christian only in frequency, degree, or length of experience.*

An antidote for doubt is found in Jude 20–21. In the Greek text this is one sentence; its verb is the word *keep* (v. 21), which is surrounded by three participles. The sentence could be rearranged thus: "Begin right now, beloved, to keep yourselves in the love of God, by continually building yourselves up, by praying unceasingly, and by constantly looking for the mercy of our Lord Jesus Christ."

Edification, building upon the foundation of "your most holy faith" (see Jude 3), stands first. A precious stone in the foundation is God's love, demonstrated by the sacrifice of his Son for the sins of his people (John 3:14–17; Rom. 5:8; 1 John 4:10). The covenant blessing that flows therefrom is the forgiveness of all our iniquities (Matt. 26:28; Eph. 1:7; Heb. 8:12). The words "and [you will] hurl all our iniquities into the depths of the sea" (Mic. 7:19) are the basis of Andrew Bonar's reflection: "May we stand upon the shore of that ocean into which our sins have been cast, and see them sink to the depths, out of sight, and the sea calm and peaceful, the sunshine playing on it, the sunshine of Thy love and Thy favor."

Jude also urges effective prayer. To pray "in the Holy Spirit" (v. 20) brings life to the soul drowning in doubt. For this is prayer with divine assistance, articulation, fervor, favor (Rom. 8:26–27), assurance of God's love, and confidence in our adoption as God's very own (Rom. 5:5; 8:15).

Jude then demands the expectation of the mercy of our Lord Jesus Christ to bring you to eternal life" (v. 21). This mercy he sends to us in this world (Pss. 23:6; 27:13–14; Heb. 4:14–16) and the next (Pss. 23:6b; 73:24; John 17:24).

To those who occupy positions of leadership among his people, let us deal with doubt severely in our personal lives. Then let us exercise the patience and compassion of Christ toward those whom we are bound to help. "Be merciful to those who doubt" (Jude 22).

Part 2

Assurance

7

Fear Not

R. C. Sproul

We are fragile mortals, given to fears of every sort. We have a built-in insecurity that no amount of whistling in the dark can mollify. We seek assurance concerning the things that frighten us the most.

The prohibition uttered most frequently by our Lord is the command, "Fear not." He said this so often to his disciples and others he encountered that it almost came to sound like a greeting. Where most people greet others by saying "Hi" or "Hello," the first words of Jesus often were "Fear not."

Why? Perhaps Jesus' predilection for those words grew out of his acute sense of the thinly veiled fear that grips all who approach the living God. We fear his power, we fear his wrath, and most of all we fear his ultimate rejection.

The assurance we need most is the assurance of salvation. Though we are loathe to think much about it or contemplate it deeply, we know, if only intuitively, that the worst catastrophe that could ever befall us is to be visited by God's final punitive wrath. Our insecurity is worsened by the certainty that we deserve it.

Many believe that assurance of eternal salvation is neither possible or even to be sought. To claim such assurance is considered a mask of supreme arrogance, the nadir of self-conceit.

Yet, if God declares that it is possible to have full assurance of salvation and even commands that we seek after it, then it would be supremely arrogant to deny our need or neglect the search.

In fact, God does command us to make our election and calling sure: *Therefore, my brothers, be all the more eager to make your calling and election sure. For if you do these things, you will never fall"* (2 Pet. 1:10).

This command admits of no justifiable neglect. It addresses a crucial matter. The question, "Am I saved?" is one of the most important I can ever ask myself. I need to know the answer; I *must* know the answer. This is not a trifle. Without the assurance of salvation the Christian life is unstable, vulnerable to the debilitating rigors of mood changes. Basing assurance on changing emotions allows the wolf of heresy to camp on the doorstep. Progress in sanctification requires a firm foundation in faith. Assurance is the cement of that foundation. Without it the foundation crumbles.

How, then, do we receive assurance? The Scripture declares that the Holy Spirit bears witness with our spirit that we are the children of God. This inner testimony of the Holy Spirit is as vital as it is complex. It can be subjected to severe distortions, being confused with subjectivism and self-delusion.

The Spirit gives his testimony *with* the Word and *through* the Word, never *without* the Word or *against* the Word.

Since it is possible to have false assurance of salvation it is all the more urgent that we seek the Spirit's testimony in and through the Word. False assurance usually proceeds from a faulty understanding of salvation. If one fails to understand the necessary conditions for salvation, assurance becomes, at best, a guess.

Therefore, we insist that right doctrine is a crucial element in acquiring a sound basis for assurance. It may even be a necessary condition, though it is by no means a sufficient condition. Without sound doctrine we will have an inadequate understanding of salvation. However, having a sound understanding of salvation is no guarantee that we have the salvation we so soundly understand.

If we think the Bible teaches universal salvation we may arrive at a false sense of assurance by reasoning as follows:

Everybody is saved.
I am a body.
∴ Therefore, I am saved.

> *Real assurance rests on a sound understanding of salvation, a sound understanding of justification, a sound understanding of sanctification, and a sound understanding of ourselves.*

Or, if we think salvation is gained by our own good works and we are further deluded into believing that we possess good works, we will have a false assurance of salvation.

To have sound assurance we must understand that our salvation rests upon the merit of Christ alone, which is appropriated to us when we embrace him by genuine faith. If we understand that, the remaining question is, "Do I have the genuine faith necessary for salvation?"

To answer that question two more things must be understood and analyzed properly. The first is doctrinal. We need a clear understanding of what constitutes genuine saving faith. If we conceive of saving faith as a faith that exists in a vacuum, never yielding the fruit of works of obedience, we have confused saving faith with dead faith, which cannot save anyone.

The second requirement involves a sober analysis of our own lives. We must examine ourselves to see if the fruit of regeneration is apparent in us. Do we have a real affection for the biblical Christ? Only the regenerate person possesses real love for the real Jesus. Next we must ask the tough question, "Does my life manifest the fruit of sanctification?" I test my faith by my works.

I call this last question the tough question for various reasons. We can lose assurance if we think perfect obedience is the test. Every sin we commit after conversion can cast doubt upon our assurance. That doubt is exacerbated by Satan's assault of accusation against us. Satan delights in shaking the true Christian's assurance.

Or we can delude ourselves by looking at our own works with an exalted view of our goodness, seeing virtue in ourselves when there is none. Here we quake in terror before our Lord's warning: *"Many will say to me on that day, 'Lord, Lord, did we not prophesy in your name, and in your name drive out demons and perform many miracles?' Then I will tell them plainly, 'I never knew you. Away from me, you evildoers!'"* (Matt. 7:22–23).

Real assurance rests on a sound understanding of salvation, a sound understanding of justification, a sound understanding of sanctification, and a sound understanding of ourselves. In all these matters we have the comfort and assistance of the Holy Spirit who illumines the text of Scripture for us, who works in us to yield the fruit of sanctification, and who bears witness with our spirit that we are the children of God.

8

The Privilege of Assurance

Roger Nicole

The privilege of assurance is secured by the work of Christ for his own; that fact is properly undergirded in the Reformed faith. Where the work of Christ is not properly understood or taught, the foundation for assurance is damaged or even destroyed.

When justification by faith alone is not duly proclaimed, the good works of the believer must be presented as at least part of the basis by which salvation is secured. But if works must participate the assurance of faith receives a fatal blow.

The prime example of this distortion is found in the official doctrine of the Roman Catholic Church as prevalent in the time of the Reformation and codified at the Council of Trent (1545–63). This view does not deny that Christ has accomplished a saving work for humanity, but justification is envisioned as the total process by which the redeemed are brought to perfection by the Holy Spirit.

For a Roman Catholic to say, "I am justified" is equivalent to making a claim of having achieved perfection. Who can realistically make such a claim? Nobody. Those who venture to do it are adjudged to be arrogant and presumptuous. The best one can say is, "I am in the process of being saved; I hope that at the end of my life I may be in a state of grace and therefore not cast into hell. I am diligently seeking to take advantage of the means of grace (sacraments) and to refrain from sinning, but only God knows whether I am going to make it."

This uncertainty drove Martin Luther almost out of his mind before he came to understand the great truth of justification by faith alone. At last he perceived that salvation is not secured through the exertion of good works, fastings, alms, and other disciplines. It has been purchased in full by the saving work of Jesus Christ, with whom we are united through faith alone. The fact of this union brings with it assurance, just as an authentic receipt brings complete release from the burden of a debt.

The Roman Church is not the only offender in this respect; many groups and individuals have clouded the pure doctrine of justification by introducing an element of human merit to the process. Even many Lutherans, otherwise orthodox, have shown reluctance to confess the perseverance of God with the redeemed, making present assurance no guarantee of ultimate salvation.

This problem also burdens the Arminian view, which is now the dominant theology among evangelical denominations. In keeping with Arminian principles that salvation is an individual's choice and may be lost through rebellion, a believer may properly say, "I am saved now," for by virtue of the work of Christ God confers salvation to any and all who repent and believe. Yet this blessing is not a basis for complete confidence that a change of disposition will not occur. There are many tragic examples, they say, of people who, after having been saved, turn away and lose out altogether. The disciple Judas is a notable case in point, and Hebrews 6:4–6 surely provides a solemn warning in this respect:

> It is impossible for those who have once been enlightened, who have tasted the heavenly gift, who have shared in the Holy Spirit, who have tasted the goodness of the word of God and the powers of the coming age, if they fall away, to be brought back to repentance, because to their loss they are crucifying the Son of God all over again and subjecting him to public disgrace.

Our salvation has been purchased in full by the saving work of Jesus Christ, with whom we are united through faith alone. The fact of this union brings with it assurance, just as an authentic receipt brings complete release from the burden of a debt.

If salvation, once experienced, is not secured by the grace of God so as to be a permanent blessing, the momentary assurance of it is of relatively small significance. Even those who, in Arminian terms, have experienced "Christian perfection" are not immune from the danger of falling from grace and being lost.

Although Arminians seldom reason this way, it would appear that the best thing that could happen would be to die as soon as one accepts Christ. To continue to live is to expose oneself to the risk of losing salvation. This is certainly not Paul's outlook in Phil. 1:22–26:

> *Assurance is grounded in the adequacy of the work of Christ, in the testimony of the Holy Spirit, and in the persistent purpose of God.*

If I am to go on living in the body, this will mean fruitful labor for me. Yet what shall I choose? I do not know! I am torn between the two: I desire to depart and be with Christ, which is better by far; but it is more necessary for you that I remain in the body. Convinced of this, I know that I will remain, and I will continue with all of you for your progress and joy in the faith, so that through my being with you again your joy in Christ Jesus will overflow on account of me.

There are, of course, other systems of thought that undermine assurance in a more fundamental way. For instance, those who deny the reality of life beyond the grave have no place for salvation, let alone assurance. Neither can those have assurance who think of salvation in social rather than individual terms. Those, finally, who expect that ultimately all rational creatures, or at least all members of the human race, will be saved extend assurance to all. But in this process they emasculate the gospel and depart from the clear teaching of Scripture as it has been well understood over the centuries.

In the Reformed doctrine assurance is grounded in the adequacy of the work of Christ, our Mediator and covenant Head, in the testimony of the Holy Spirit who witnesses with our spirit that we are children of God (Rom. 8:16), and in the persistent purpose of God who has begun a good work in the believer and will carry it to completion until the day of Christ (Phil. 1:6).

9

True and False Assurance

John Gerstner

Probably Romans 8:16 is the greatest assurance text in the entire Bible. It is appealed to by Reformed and Arminian evangelicals alike, though they have conflicting ideas of assurance.

Romans 8:16 reads, "The Spirit himself testifies with our spirit that we are God's children." Arminians say this means that true Christians do have true assurance of a present, but, losable salvation. The Reformed view says that what the Holy Spirit and the Christian's spirit testify to is a present assurance of unlosable eternal life. One of these views certainly is false, and one may be true.

The text itself, on the surface, does not settle this difference. It only says that *his* Spirit and *our* spirit testify to our being (at the moment) children of God. Arminian and Calvinist agree on that: The text itself only asserts a present experience. So we agree on what the text says and differ on the context and implications of what it says.

The Arminian view says that the Christian can and does have assurance of true eternal salvation but may lose that salvation. If the Holy Spirit testifies along with the spirit the Christian has eternal life—at that moment. The believer may, however, sin so as to lose that salvation at any future moment. Because the Arminian can *never be sure* before death that such fall(s) may not occur, the Arminian can never have more than momentary assurance of eternal life until he or she enters heaven and for the first time *has* assurance of eternal life. Nevertheless and alas, according to the Arminian view of "free will," the individual cannot have assurance of eternal life even in heaven. As long as "free will" exists, and the Arminian considers free will essential to human nature, the individual must be able to choose for *or against* God.

Can the Arminian have assurance? Obviously not on Arminian principles. Even as the Spirit is testifying with the believer's spirit, the Arminian knows that his or her free will may reject the Holy Spirit *even while the Spirit is testifying.* True, the believer may not reject the Spirit, but who knows? Surely not the human being who must always be free to change his or her mind. Not even God can be sure whether the Arminian will be saved because if God knew *beforehand*, this Arminian would not be "free" to change. If the mind does change, God's knowledge "beforehand" would be proven false.

Some Arminians try to keep their theology and escape this charge. They say, God's knowing beforehand does not *determine* the will and thus destroy personal freedom. However, it destroys the freedom the Arminian affirms, because something being certain beforehand means that the man or woman will not, and therefore cannot, choose otherwise. Thus, the individual cannot be free and human in an evangelical understanding of things.

The Arminian cannot have assurance for one moment, though the Holy Spirit himself is testifying at this moment that this Christian is a child of God. There always must be the option to reject the Holy Spirit's testimony at any moment. *The Arminian, therefore, cannot, on Arminian principles, have assurance of even momentary salvation, not to mention eternal salvation.*

The Arminian interpretation thus destroys the testimony of Romans 8:16. An Arminian evangelical who claims even momentary assurance of salvation is a living contradiction. Anyone true to *this* evangelicalism cannot have assurance. Anyone who has assurance is not an Arminian.

The Reformed view says that what the Holy Spirit and the Christian's spirit testify to is a present assurance of unlosable eternal life.

Let us now consider the Reformed understanding of Romans 8:16 and assurance. Reformed Christians believe no one comes to Christ unless drawn by the Holy Spirit and that, once drawn, justified, and made holy with the righteousness of Jesus, the Christian can never be plucked from his Lord's hand. A Reformed Christian claims the text teaches that the Christian has a testimony of the divine and human spirits to the Christian's eternal salvation. This is an impossibility on Arminian

principles, but it is compatible with Reformed principles; in
fact this assurance grows out of them. If there were no Romans
8:16 one could still deduce this concept of salvation from many
other texts.

Children of God (8:16) are heirs of God and joint-heirs
with Christ forever (8:17) and cannot fall because they never
cease to be the children of God. Arminians deny that this is
possible. Only two historic theologies make any serious claim
to being biblical in regards to this text, the Reformed and
the Arminian evangelical. The Reformed view affirms perseverance of the saints and the Arminian view denies it. Armini-
anism fails because its own principles make even a *momentary* testimony of the Holy Spirit impossible. Reformed
principles, in contrast, are perfectly harmonious with a testimony of the Holy Spirit because they teach that, once a person is born again, that seed never dies and so remains in essential harmony with the Holy Spirit who begot it and with his
testimony.

This concurrent testimony does occur, and it will never
change—except for the better. Furthermore, it must be a joint
testimony to eternal life, giving the regenerate soul assurance
of persevering in eternal life.

10

Assurance and Sin

Ron Kilpatrick

"Put a tiger in your tank" advocated the old TV commercial. A tiger was shown leaping into the engine of a car. The hood clanked shut, and the car thundered off. The graphic suggestion was that the right gasoline would add the ferocity of a tiger to your engine, making for pick-up, power, and speed.

Evangelical author Leslie Flynn, in an essay on "What Sin Does to Us," describes the filming of this commercial to illustrate the havoc sin wreaks in a Christian's life.

A Detroit advertising agency was hired to film what turned out to be a harrowing commercial. First, they secured a tiger named Patty and hired a film crew. The body of a car, minus the engine, was placed over a shallow pit. It would certainly be an easy matter to entice the tiger to leap through the empty engine compartment and into the pit.

But Patty refused to jump. For days they tried to coax her. A trainer held juicy chunks of raw beef down in the pit, to no avail. Finally, as a last tactic, the trainer climbed into the pit with live chickens. The chickens squawked. The cameras whirred. The tiger made a perfect leap into the open engine and down into the pit, emerging later in a flurry of feathers.

Imagine being tiger bait. Too many unwary Christians do not heed the apostle Peter's warning that a "roaring lion" is on the prowl (1 Peter 5:8). Satan, of course, is the lion, but we also should beware a "tiger"—sin that remains in our fallen nature. This tiger is not in the tank but in the heart, continually stalking the child of God. We can no more control sin than the trainer could command Patty, and it is just as bloodthirsty. When we neglect the Source of our righteousness and try to master the beast on our own, the joy and peace we should feel as a child of God end up as a mouthful of feathers.

The roaring lion and his stalking tiger can be overcome. Flynn concludes, "The Lion of the tribe of Judah, who came to earth as the Lamb of God, can conquer and control our fallen nature."

Under such a conquering Lord, why should we continue to play a game of chicken with the tiger? A little candid self-assessment can probably identify a few reasons. But behind most excuses for Christian entrapment lies one ominous attitude: We value God's grace so cheaply that the rules no longer seem to apply. We are like the woman who told her pastor, "Well, after all, sin is different for a Christian than for an unbeliever."

We need to hear her pastor's wise reply: "You're right, it's worse."

It is worse, not only because sin is a personal affront to the Lord who bought the Christian, but also because it devastates the life and witness of the believer. Backsliding can cause us to lose our blessed assurance and plunge us into spiritual depression.

Backsliding describes the state of the believer whose spiritual life declines until spiritual vitality is lost through deliberate disobedience to the Lord. It consists of faithlessly turning or drawing back from what the Lord demands (Jer. 3:6–14; Hosea 11:7).

When true believers lapse into sins, whether the heinous crimes of David and Peter or habitual "little" sins, they may suffer the loss of the inward assurance they once knew. And they may cry out with the Psalmist, "Lord, why do You cast off my soul? Why do You hide Your face from me?" (Ps. 88:14 NKJV).

Behind most excuses for Christian entrapment lies one ominous attitude: We value God's grace so cheaply that the rules no longer seem to apply.

This loss of assurance is twice portrayed in John Bunyan's great work, *Pilgrim's Progress*. When Christian and Hopeful disobey their instructions, leave the path to the Celestial City, and climb over the fence, they face a terrible storm. Then they are caught by Giant Despair and thrust into the dungeon of Doubting Castle. Here they languish until Christian realizes he has the key of God's promises that will bring release and restoration. The Westminster Confession of Faith and Larger and Shorter Catechisms speak of the real peril of true believers losing their assurance through sinful rebellion in the following terms. Question 81 of the Larger Catechism states clearly this relationship between lost assurance and continuing sin:

> Assurance of grace and salvation not being of the essence of faith, true believers may wait long before they obtain it, and after the enjoyment thereof, may have it weakened and intermitted, through manifold distempers, sins, temptation, and desertions; yet are they never left without such a presence and support of the Spirit of God as keeps them from sinking into utter despair.

Bishop of Liverpool J. C. Ryle, in his classic work *Holiness* (Revell repr., 1979, p. 125) warned his readers about the possibility of this dire loss and exhorted them to take pains to guard and preserve it:

> Do not forget that assurance is a thing which may be lost for a season, even by the brightest Christians, unless they take care.
>
> Assurance is a most delicate plant. It needs daily, hourly watching, watering, tending, cherishing. So watch and pray the more when you have got it. As [Samuel] Rutherford says, "Make much of assurance." Be always upon your guard. . . . Keep that in mind. . . .
>   Spiritual darkness comes on horseback, and goes away on foot. It is upon us before we know that it is coming. It leaves us slowly, gradually, and not until after many days. It is easy to run downhill. It is hard work to climb up. So remember my caution—when you have the joy of the Lord, watch and pray.
>
> Above all, grieve not the Spirit. Quench not the Spirit. Vex not the Spirit. Drive Him not to a distance by tampering with small bad habits and little sins. Little jarrings between hus-

bands and wives make unhappy homes. Petty inconsistencies, known and allowed, will bring a strangeness in between you and the Spirit.

This rare jewel of Christian contentment or blessed assurance may be lost by a believer. The real possibility of this loss and the causes of it are further spelled out by the American Presbyterian theologian John Murray in Banner of Truth's *Collected Works* (1978, 2:266):

> In other cases, however, the absence of full assurance is due to . . . disobedience to the commandments of God, backsliding, unwatchfulness, prayerlessness, excessive care for the things of this life, and worldliness. There are many sins which believers are prone to indulge and cause to stumble, with the result that their Father's displeasure is manifest in the withdrawing of the light of his countenance, so that they are bereft of the joy of their salvation. Those who at one time enjoyed this assurance may lose it.

The good news is that it is possible to recover the lost treasure of assurance. The God of the second chance can "restore to you the years that the swarming locust has eaten" (Joel 2:25, NKJV). The Lord can "give them beauty for ashes, the oil of joy for mourning, the garment of praise for the spirit of heaviness; That they might be called trees of righteousness, the planting of the LORD that He may be glorified" (Isa. 61:3, NKJV). The secret to the restoration of assurance is expressed well by John White in his book, *The Fight: A Practical Handbook to Christian Living* (1976, pp. 88–89):

> The Father does not welcome you because you have been trying hard, because you have made a thorough going confession, or because you have been making spiritual strides

recently. He does not welcome you because you have something you can be proud about. He welcomes you because His Son died for you.

Therefore, when you find the grey cloud descending, whether it be as you pray, as you work, as you testify or whatever, when you find the ring of assurance going from your words because of a vague sense of guilt, look up to God and say, "Thank you, my Father, for the blood of your Son. Thank you, even now, that you accept me gladly, lovingly in spite of all I am and have done—because of His death. Father and God, I come.

Two centuries ago there was an English clergyman named Robert Robinson. In addition to his gifts as a pastor and preacher, he was an accomplished poet and hymn writer. After many years in the ministry he began to drift in his spiritual life. He left the ministry and traveled to France where he sank further into sin and lost his assurance. One night he was riding in a carriage with a Parisian socialite who had recently become a believer. She was reading some poetry to him and asked, "And what do you think of this one?":

> Come thou Fount of every blessing,
> Tune my heart to sing thy grace.
> Streams of mercy never failing
> Call for hymns of loudest praise.

> ["Come Thou Fount of Every Blessing"]

When she looked over at him she noticed that he was crying.

"What do I think of it?" he asked in a broken voice. "I wrote it; but now I've drifted away from him and can't find my way back."

"But don't you see?" said the woman quietly, "The way back is written right here in the third line of your poem: 'Streams of mercy never ceasing'—Those streams are flowing even here in Paris tonight."

Robinson recommitted his life to Christ and regained his blessed assurance. That streams of mercy ever flow for the wayward Christian is the vital difference between the child of God and those chickens in the tiger pit. We may not feel very sure of our salvation—nor should we—after we have made light of the infinite cost of the cross.

But God's promise remains eternal, unshaken by our foolish toying with tigers. Mercy is extended toward us sinners in the strong paw of the Lion of Judah.

11

How to Know That You Know Him

Steve Brown

The nature of the God of the universe is not to bring you to a saving knowledge of Jesus Christ, then to make you wonder for the rest of your life whether or not you have a saving knowledge of Jesus Christ. God does not say, "Trust me," then for the rest of your life make you wonder if you really trust him.

It is his business and desire for us to have assurance of salvation. How do you know that you know him? Check out five indicators from the writer of Hebrews 6:

1. The *direction* in which your life is going.
2. The *love* your life is showing.

3. The *service* your life is sharing.
4. The *concern* for godliness you are feeling.
5. The *longing* in your desire for fellowshiping.

First, if you are looking for assurance check out your life. The writer of Hebrews casts sobering words at those who inhabit the fringes of faith, desiring to taste but never receiving God's mercy and producing weeds instead of fruits in their lives. The believer's life, however, holds a far more positive promise:

> Even though we speak like this, dear friends, we are confident of better things in your case—things that accompany salvation. God is not unjust; he will not forget your work and the love you have shown him as you have helped his people and continue to help them. We want each of you to show this same diligence to the very end in order to make your hope sure. We do not want you to become lazy, but to imitate those who through faith and patience inherit what has been promised [Heb. 6:9–12].

Most people think that God looks at where you are along the road of life. We do that, but God doesn't. God asks only two things: First, he wants to know from where you have come; second he wants to know the direction in which you are going. In other words, I might be a lot more terrible than you, but the point is that we are moving in the same direction. You are just further down the road than I am. God's pleasure and our assurance come from moving in that right direction. That is how the writer of Hebrews could look at his hearers and be "confident of better things in your case—things that accompany salvation" (vs. 9b).

If you were to wake up tomorrow morning to discover that God does not exist, what difference would it make in your life? I would be devastated. A lot that is happening in my life would be wiped out. If you do not have an answer to that question, aside from the fact that you would not attend church once a week, then you need to read 6:4–8 once again. According to this passage you may have a serious problem.

One time a pastor friend of mine was talking to a girl in New England who had recently become a Christian. She was very angry and bitter. She asked, "Why do I have to go through all this hurt? Why is there all this pain in the world? Why do I have all these problems?"

My friend asked a classic question: "Would you rather not have known him?"

It is God's desire that his people come into a relationship with the Father that is so close we know and feel secure with him.

She understood. As she thought about her answer to that question she found assurance of her relationship with Jesus Christ.

Second, in looking for assurance you should check out your love. Look again at verse 10: "God is not unjust; he will not forget your work and the love you have shown him as you have helped his people and continue to help them."

The writer of Hebrews is not just talking about a tingle up your spine or a wonderful love song. He is talking about love in action, the kind of love you show to the saints for his sake. Love is not a noun; it is a verb. What do you do to show love for someone else? When you give a cup of cold water in the name of Christ, regardless of how you feel about that person, the giving is in love. When you reach out to a brother or sister who is in need, no matter how you feel about them, that is love, too. The writer of Hebrews is saying that you, as a Christian, have a love that you have *shown*, not that you have *felt*. This is a sign of your relationship with Christ, for that is an indication of your relationship with Christ in your Christlikeness:

> Greater love has no one than this, that he lay down his life for his friends [John 15:13].

> You see, at just the right time, when we were still powerless, Christ died for the ungodly [Rom. 5:6].

Love is action! Are you acting in obedience to him, showing love to your brothers and sisters? If you are you are on the road to assurance.

Third, make sure to check out your level—the level of a servant.

We spent a lot of years in Massachusetts. At least at that time they believed that having a driver's license is not a right; it is a privilege. So, if the head of the Department of Motor Vehicles decides you are guilty of some offense, whether you are guilty or not, the director can take your license away from you, and you don't have any recourse.

When you and I became Christians, at that point we gave up *every* right. We are servants. As a Christian you have privileges, but you should not presume on those privileges. If your Christian faith is used to manipulate other people it is not the real thing. If your Christian faith is a vehicle for being a master it is not the real thing. Jesus said, "Whoever wants to become great among you must be your servant" (Matt. 20:26).

When you see yourself willing to be a servant, willing not to take the credit, willing to just stand behind someone else and make them great, then you are on the road to assurance.

Fourth, if you are looking for assurance of your salvation, check out your liveliness. Hebrews 6:11 speaks of the author's desire for "each of you to show this same diligence to the very end in order to make your hope sure." We might call this diligence *earnestness* to realize full assurance. When people asked Charles Spurgeon how they could know if they were of the elect he would answer: "If you are worried about it, then you are."

Now, if you have been struggling with assurance, plagued with the constant thought that "I may not really belong to God," the very fact that you are earnestly concerned is a good sign that you may belong to him, when that earnestness stands alongside other evidence of the fruits of the Spirit.

You may remember the demonstration of Solomon's wisdom in 1 Kings 3:16–28. Two women were brought to him, both claiming to be the mother of one baby. Each of the mothers had had a baby. One of the babies was dead. One mother said to Solomon, "Her baby died, and at night she switched her dead baby for my live one." The second mother made the same accusation. So they came to Solomon, asking him to determine to whom the baby really belonged. Solomon had one of his servants take a sword and hold the baby up. Then Solomon said, "Cut the living child in two and give half to one and half to the other." While one of the mothers agreed that his idea sounded reasonable, the other said, "No! Don't do that. Give the baby to her." Solomon at that point exercised a principle built into the very nature of things, so that he knew who was the real mother.

The principle was this: Concern is manifested in direct proportion to how much you care.

The same principle works to help you know about your relationship with God. If you are concerned about your relationship with Christ, if you are earnest about it or diligent, that is an indication that you are in Christ. You are on the road to assurance.

Fifth, if you are looking for assurance, check out your longing. The writer of Hebrews is saying: "I desire that you come to the point at which you know that you know that you know that you know." There are those who say you can never know. They say the only way you can get assurance is to die and find out whether your feet are cold.

If you have heard and believed that, you have believed a lie. It is God's desire that his people come into a relationship with the Father that is so close we know and feel secure with him.

I have a friend who adopted a teenager who had been shifted from foster home to foster home. When I first visited them I noticed that this boy was jumping to do everything possible to please his new parents. He made up his bed. He wanted to dry dishes and to vacuum the rug. Whenever a teenager gets *that* good I get uncomfortable. Something is wrong.

I didn't understand it at first, but then I thought about what that boy had been through. He had been kicked out of so many homes, and he was going to hang onto this one by being good.

A year later I visited the home and saw the teenager again. He was the most secure young man I have ever seen. He was relaxed and normal. He had to be nudged to do the things he was supposed to do. What happened? He had achieved assurance, assurance that this mom and dad were not going to kick him out.

We are like that. Maybe right now you are working very hard at being obedient because you don't have assurance. Maybe right now you are scared that you are not really a Christian. What should you do about that in order to have assurance? My advice is to persevere and "keep on truckin'." One day you will be so tired of obedience, so tired of holding on with a grip that makes your knuckles turn white. Then you will let go.

At that moment you will make a wonderful discovery: He was holding you all along. You will know that you know him. And that is called "assurance."

12

Assurance

A Pastor's Perspective

John Richard DeWitt

What does a pastor think about assurance? By assurance here I mean the certainty that through Jesus Christ one is a child of God: forgiven, renewed, having eternal life. I cannot speak for others, but I can give my thoughts on the subject, observations that are based on more than thirty years of ministry.

As a pastor I am committed to the welfare of the congregation I serve and want the people to whom I minister to be in good spiritual health. This means, of course, that the whole matter of assurance is very important to me. If people lack assurance they will not be whole, and they are bound to lack the joy and peace which are so essential to a mature Christian experience.

I have to say at the same time, however, that I am far more concerned about some other matters than I am about a lack of assurance. There have been times in the past when a want of assurance among serious, spiritually-minded men and women was pervasive. Generally speaking, that is seldom the case now. For many people spiritual health and the state of their souls are nonissues. If I were to begin to encounter people genuinely troubled by doubts about their salvation I should regard it as a healthy sign.

Problems with respect to assurance may arise for any number of reasons.

It should be said at once that personality differences play a considerable part. Optimistic, positive, confident people are far less prone to introspection and doubt about themselves than are those whose inclination it is to look on the dark side of things and who are by nature introspective. It is essential that we understand this and that we do not regard everyone in the same light. One who has struggled much and gone through deep valleys will be much more likely to ask questions in this area than another who has encountered few or no inner conflicts. I do not suggest, of course, that the one type of personality is more spiritual than the other; I only point out that people differ.

Further, many folk, within as well as outside the church, have no right whatsoever to assurance. They are not believers. They have not experienced true conversion. They may suppose that all is well, but it is not, and we do them no favor by allowing them to continue in their delusion. Some in this category may be "awakened" but not yet "converted." They have, perhaps, come to grasp something of the seriousness of their position outside of Jesus Christ, but they have not yet come to faith in him. To try to rush them out of conviction and into an easy assurance commits a grievous error.

Others, in my experience, have fallen into sin. They feel defeated and question, in guilt, their relationship to God. They may even begin to doubt the very existence of God and the truth of the gospel. It is, for many, easier to deny that God is than to acknowledge failure and to repent.

Sometimes physical or emotional illness may be the reason for spiritual uncertainty. I have observed that those who are not well—whose physical or mental constitution is under attack by illness—are prone to depression and often experience uneasiness about their relationship with God. They may lose hope and even begin to believe that God has abandoned them. These sufferers are frequently helped by being reminded of the connection between illness and feelings. In certain cases a pastor can do great good by referring a troubled person to a skilled physician. People with healthy bodies and healthy minds have far fewer problems about assurance than those who are sick.

True certainty rests on the objective truth of Scripture, for there the Holy Spirit reveals God's promises, commands, and the mercy bestowed to broken individuals who respond in committed belief and repentance.

In other instances people may be in difficulty with respect to assurance because of bad teaching in the church. The doctrine of predestination is not set forth in the Bible to produce spiritual anxiety. On the contrary, it is intended to strengthen, to edify, to encourage. "If God is for us, who can be against us?" (Rom. 8:31). If this great truth is distorted, people are led to wonder whether they are elect. If one cannot know that one is elect, how can one know that one is a child of God? Clearly the answer here is to gain an understanding of what the Bible actually teaches.

Under different circumstances, however, a radically different kind of teaching may lead people to think that nothing more is involved in becoming a Christian than to "make a decision for Christ." Across the Christian world spiritual birth or conversion has been placed almost on the level of a mathematical formula. That formula might be stated something like this:

> When the invitation is given, go forward. If you go forward and sincerely repeat the words of a prayer of confession and faith, if you sign the commitment card, then [so we are told] you are a Christian. You may not feel like one, act like one, or have any substantial ground for considering yourself one. Nevertheless, if you have made a decision for Christ, that is all you need do. And beyond that, you have the right to regard yourself as a fully assured child of God.

I am much more concerned about this "easy believism" notion that one can be a Christian without displaying any vital signs of spiritual life than I am about an absence of assurance. One cannot know Jesus Christ as Savior and not know him in some emerging way as Lord and Master of one's life. Our objective must be to return to the teaching of Scripture, to be faithful to the Word of God in setting forth the plan of salvation without cutting corners and giving people false grounds for assurance.

All who are called upon to give spiritual counsel must be wise and faithful when attempting to discern whether an individual lacks assurance—or repentance. It is tempting to give the same answer, whatever the question, but anything of that sort is quite wrong. Simple formulae ignore differences among people and the diverse causes of spiritual anxiety. Wise physicians of the soul are never content to treat all cases in the same manner. Intricate matters of the soul need more than a prescription of easy answers.

The ultimate response to doubting hearts—our own and the hearts of others—must be to look to Jesus, who knew those he met more personally than ever we could. A rich man came seeking easy assurance, and Jesus sent him away in sorrow. A Samaritan woman came more broken than she knew and he gave her more than she knew to request. A repentant Peter found fresh assurance in a renewed commission: "Feed my sheep." An overconfident moralist named Paul was utterly struck down so he could be utterly remade.

Assurance must never be built upon shortcuts to grace or emotions that rise and fall, the sorts of empty certitudes passed out in many churches. Healing assurance that honestly deals with my doubts . . . and needs . . . takes into account who I am and how holy God truly is. Confidence grows through intimacy with my Father and Lord, trusting him and confronting sins before his throne. True certainty rests on the objective truth of Scripture, for there the Holy Spirit reveals God's promises, commands, and the mercy bestowed to broken individuals who respond in committed belief and repentance.

Epilogue

R. C. Sproul

After Blaise Pascal died in 1662 his servant discovered a small piece of parchment sewn into the doublet that had belonged to the mathematician and Christian thinker. At the top of the paper Pascal had drawn a cross. Beneath the cross were these words:

In the year of the Lord 1654
Monday, November 23
From about half-past ten in the evening
until half-past twelve.

Fire

God of Abraham, God of Isaac, God of Jacob
Not of the philosophers nor of the scholars.
Certainty. Joy. Certainty, feeling, joy, peace . . .

The Sublimity of the Human Soul

Just Father, the world has not known thee
but I have known thee.

Joy, joy, joy, tears of joy.
I do not separate myself from thee. . . .

Pascal's "Night of Fire" was an experience that gripped his
soul and changed the course of his life. He kept the record of
it literally close to his heart. The resounding theme of his
record was one of joy—a sublime joy accompanied by peace.

Coupled to his echo of joy is the word *certainty*. His sublime joy was linked inseparably to some kind of assurance.

Joy is the result of assurance. It is the assurance, not merely
of God's existence that yields such joy, but his divine favor and
compassion. To know that we are his is the rock upon which
sublime joy rests.

A "Night of Fire" settled something in Pascal's soul, once
and for all time. To gain assurance of our redemption is to
get our lives settled. Once assurance is attained, doubt exits
from the soul—and joy rushes in to fill the vacuum.

It is a quest worth the journey.

For Reflection and Discussion

Chapter 1 **The Anatomy of Doubt**

1. According to American humorist Josh Billings, "It is better to know nothing than to know what ain't so." To declare with all your might that something is true, only to find out it just "ain't so" is a common but embarrassing experience. How can you know when it is wiser to be a play-it-safe Erasmus than an asserting Luther?

2. What distinguishes "authentic doubt" from a rebellious skepticism that assails the heart?

3. What would life be like for an utterly consistent skeptic, who refused to accept the necessity of cause and effect or the laws of logic?

4. Where can we go for "first principles that are certain" when struggling with faith assailing doubt? Can those principles include confidence that there is a God? . . . that he is sufficient? . . . that he has revealed himself?

Read Hebrews 1:1–3, thinking of ways God once revealed himself. Has Jesus Christ become a final, sufficient source of confidence in your life?

Chapter 2 When Doubt Becomes Unbelief

1. C. S. Lewis's demon in *The Screwtape Letters* said it well: "Our cause is never more in danger than when a human . . . looks round upon a universe from which every trace of Him seems to have vanished, and asks why he has been forsaken, and still obeys." Can you "learn to be relaxed about doubt" when every trace of God seems missing from your universe?

2. Is it wrong to long for certainty in matters of faith? What is faith if "the atheist's belief that there is no God is just as much a matter of faith as your belief that there is"?

3. Look again at Alister McGrath's definition of *unbelief* on page 22. Can a Christian, like the unbeliever, live as if there is no God?

4. What tricks has Satan used to break your links with God? Have you experienced any of the three possible routes by which unbelief comes? How do you stop allowing doubt to dominate?

5. Read Ephesians 4:11–15. What principles on page 24 and in this passage help you avoid the pitfalls of unbelief?

Chapter 3 Doubt and the Apologist

1. "Always be prepared," said the apostle Peter, "to give an answer to everyone who asks you to give the reason for the hope that you have" (1 Pet. 3:15). That, ultimately, is the task of being an apologist. Does that mean that every Christian must be a C. S. Lewis style defender of the faith?

2. While we don't know for sure what Lewis's feelings were after debating Elizabeth Anscombe, how do you suppose such a Christian thinker might feel after "choking"?

3. Consider the two risks of defending the faith mentioned by W. Andrew Hoffecker. Which is more to be feared: Not having the best answer or winning the argument but losing humility?

4. Read the context of Peter's admonition in 1 Peter 3:8–17. What is the apostle's answer to the frail Christian who struggles with the fear of speaking for or living for Jesus Christ?

Chapter 4 I Believe in Doubt

1. The words mentioned by Os Guinness (p. 33) paint graphic word pictures. *Distazō*, for example, suggests a person trying to stand on two roads at one time. *Meteōrizomai* could refer to raising a sail or high fortifications. Its idea is that part of the mind floats up in the clouds. In what ways do such words describe the distraction of uncertainty?

2. How does one keep a balanced perspective on doubts, avoiding extremes of despair and unconcern? Does James 1:2–8 provide any help in properly judging doubt?

3. Should you be afraid to admit your questionings? How does that fear sometimes relate to the "major misconception" Guinness mentions on page 32?

4. Where can you go for help in dealing with confusions of mind?

5. What might be some underlying causes of uncertainty in your life?

Chapter 5 Doubt in the Face of Suffering

1. "Brother, said Christian, what shall we do? The life that we now live is miserable. For my part, I know not whether it is best to live thus, or die out of hand . . . and the grave is more easy for me than this dungeon. Shall we be ruled by this giant?" How might Sinclair Ferguson answer the question Christian asked in the dungeon of Giant Despair in *Pilgrim's Progress*?

2. What did Robert Bruce mean when he said, "It is a great thing to believe in God"?

3. Is it wrong to want instant relief or quick answers? What do we learn about God when we must wait?

4. Read the Scriptures accompanying the six observations about the nature of suffering (pp. 39–41). Why is it sometimes hard to appreciate these blessings from God?

5. What can you do to better fill your mind with Scripture so that you can speak back to your troubled soul as did the psalmists?

Chapter 6 Doubting God's Goodness

1. The Living Bible paraphrase presents an encouraging thought in Romans 8:37: "*Overwhelming victory* is ours through Christ who loved us enough to die for us" (Living Bible). But actually this verse begins: "*Despite all this* we overwhelmingly conquer. . . ." How can you reconcile victory in Christ with overwhelming difficulties some people experience each day?

2. Do you agree that "doubt is a fact of life, differing from Christian to Christian only in frequency, degree, or length of experience"?

3. What antidote for doubt is prescribed by R. Bruce Steward (p. 44)?

4. How does prayer and the expectation of mercy empower us to deal with our own doubts and to be merciful to our fellow doubters?

Chapter 7 Fear Not

1. In *Being a Christian When the Chips Are Down* Helmut Thielicke describes the Christian's assurance through Albrecht Dürer's painting "Knight, Death, and Devil." A confident knight stands alone, showing no fear, though death and demons lurk in the darkness. They have no power over him. On what basis is such assurance justified?

2. Why is it arrogant to neglect the search for full assurance of salvation?

3. What does R. C. Sproul mean in calling assurance a *cement* that holds together "a firm foundation in faith?"

4. Compare Romans 8:16 with 1 Corinthians 2:10-12 and 1 John 3:24. How can you know that the Holy Spirit is the one testifying that you are God's child?

5. What two things must you understand in order to have sound assurance of salvation (p. 52)?

Chapter 8 The Privilege of Assurance

1. A holy and just God must denounce and punish sin. God never declares guilty people innocent. Yet suddenly the prisoner who has been found guilty and sentenced learns that his or her sentence

already has been carried out on another. At what cost does God offer what Roger Nicole calls "the privilege of assurance"?

2. What are the primary differences among the Roman Catholic, Arminian, and Reformed views of justification?

3. Does Hebrews 6:4–6 teach that the Christian may become apostate and fall from grace? Refer to 1 John 2:19 for interpretive help.

4. Why is the Reformed insistence that justification is grounded only in the work of Christ so vital to assurance?

Chapter 9 Assurance and Sin

1. The Holy Spirit's ministry in the heart of a believer is the focus of Romans 8:16. That ministry must have been in George Matheson's mind when he penned:

> O Light that followest all my way,
> I yield my flick'ring torch to thee;
> My heart restores its borrowed ray,
> That in thy sunshine's blaze its day
> May brighter, fairer be.
>
> ["O Love That Wilt Not Let Me Go"]

What do these words suggest about the Holy Spirit's work in the Christian?

2. What really is the difference between the concepts of Arminian and Reformed Christians who both claim assurance of salvation?

3. Isn't the Christian free to change his or her mind and decide to reject Jesus Christ?

4. Describe the Reformed understanding of Romans 8:16 and what it means to be a child of God.

5. John Gerstner writes of a doctrine that is sometimes called *perseverance of the saints.* If sanctification makes repentant sinners into *saints* what should a persevering life look like?

Chapter 10 Assurance and Sin

1. Many Christians learn the hard way that victory over sin is not an automatic given in redeemed "saints." Look at 1 Peter 5:6–10 and its illustration of Satan as a roaring lion. In this text what does Peter tell the Christian to do? What does he promise that God will do?

2. Is the "tiger" of sin different from the "lion" Satan? Who *is* the real enemy that Ron Kilpatrick describes?

3. Sin makes the unbeliever liable for eternal punishment? Is the sin committed by a Christian in some sense worse than that?

4. If Christians never lose their salvation how is it that they sometimes lose their assurance? Can you understand why God would temporarily remove your assurance? Under what circumstances might he work in this way?

5. If you feel you have lost this treasure what steps can you take in its recovery?

Chapter 11 How to Know That You Know Him

1. Read Hebrews 6, looking for the "five indicators" by which to judge your life. Are these indicators primarily inner feelings, outward actions, or inner feelings that spill from the heart into outward actions? How can each of these indicators test whether you are merely "tasting" or fully receiving God's grace?

2. Steve Brown asserts that God doesn't look at where you are going but rather where you have come from and the direction in which you are headed (p. 74). What does he mean? Does this give some perspective in evaluating your growth?

3. Which is to be preferred: To go through life without worries and without God, or to face great difficulties in the presence of God?

4. Why has the role of servant become so unpopular in our society and even in the church? How might this indicate a prevalent problem with our fellowship with God?

5. Does your life seem more like the newly adopted teenager who felt insecure or the boy who had become confident of his place in the family?

Chapter 12 Assurance: A Pastor's Perspective

1. One controversy in the church concerns whether a person can be a Christian without submitting to the lordship of Jesus Christ. Evangelists invite people to believe Jesus is the Son of God and that he died on the cross. Pray a sinner's prayer, they say, and your ticket to heaven is punched. The decision to submit to Christ as Lord is regarded as a different matter, a decision we may make later if we are so moved. Does this lack of lordship contribute to the problem John Richard DeWitt addresses?

2. Why does DeWitt say that people who lack assurance are not whole? What happens to the body of Christ when many of its members lack a mature Christian experience?

3. How does personality affect personal assurance of salvation? Lack of belief? Habitual sin? Illness? Distorted teaching? Do some of these factors affect your assurance?

4. Why is "easy believism" a more serious problem among today's Christians than lack of assurance? What are the "vital signs of spiritual life" this writer sees missing?

5. Look at each of the foundational stones for assurance mentioned at the conclusion of this chapter. What steps can you personally take in each area to strengthen your foundation of faith?